DATE DUE			
NOV 0 - '93			
Heringes			
MY 08 '94			
OCT 18 '94			
MAR 3 1 '95			
Ochoa			

Where Animals Live

The World of Butterflies

Text by David Saintsing

Photographs by Oxford Scientific Films

Gareth Stevens Children's Books
MILWAUKEE

The Garden Butterfly

Butterflies are found in most parts of the world. Like this Swallowtail, butterflies need the sun to warm them up and make them active. This is why, in cooler places, they fly more on warm sunny days. They may even be seen north of the Arctic Circle during the short arctic summer. They are not found south of the Antarctic Circle, however.

Gardens and parks are made mainly for people, not animals. This makes gardens different from many wild *habitats*. Gardens do, however, offer food and shelter for many wild animals.

Like this Red Admiral, butterflies come into gardens to look for the nectar of flowers. Some butterflies *hibernate* in gardens for the winter.

Butterflies are insects. They spend the first part of their lives as caterpillars. They then change into adult butterflies.

Most butterflies lay their eggs outside of the garden. Some butterflies are like this Cabbage White, however. They lay their eggs in gardens. The caterpillars then hatch and feed on plants.

The Butterfly's Body

The body of a butterfly is divided into three parts. These parts are the head, the *thorax*, and the *abdomen*.

The main sense *organs* are on the head. The sense organs tell the butterfly what is happening around it. On the head are two large eyes. Each eye has thousands of little windows, or facets. Each facet is like a little eye. Together, they build up a larger picture.

The *antennae*, or feelers, stick up from the head. Butterflies use antennae to smell the air. They help butterflies look for food or other butterflies to mate with. Below the head are two *palps*. They help the butterfly sense food.

Between the two palps is the *proboscis*, or feeding tube. This Swallowtail (right) is ready to reach deep into flowers for nectar. The Cabbage White below is not using its proboscis and has coiled it up under its head.

Here you can see the large rounded eyes and sensitive antennae on this Marbled White butterfly. You can also see three of the butterfly's six jointed legs. The tip of each leg has sense organs for tasting. This means that a butterfly can taste through its feet!

The thorax is the powerhouse of the body. Along its side are small holes called *spiracles*. Instead of lungs, butterflies breathe through these holes. The heart is shaped like a tube.

The small scales on the wings overlap like roof shingles. They reflect light and give the wings their pretty colors.

The abdomen contains the digestive system and sex organs. You can see that it is divided into segments.

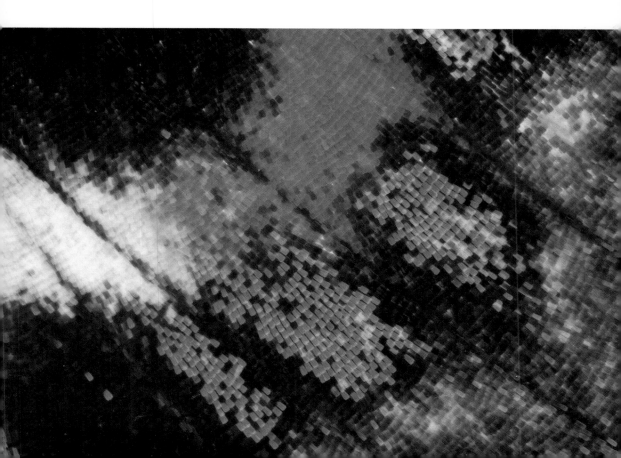

The Butterfly's Day

Each butterfly has its own way of flying. Some, like this Monarch, fly in a slow, lazy, gliding way. Butterflies can change their flight patterns if they are chased. A slow flight can turn quickly into a zig-zag.

Like this Small Copper, butterflies need the warmth of the sun to make them active. We often see them sitting in the sun with their wings stretched open.

Like many animals, butterflies have a *territory* that they treat as their own. This Hedge Brown, or Gatekeeper, flies up and down fields to claim its territory.

Some butterflies, like the Alfalfa in North America, do not claim territories. Instead, they roam all about to look for food or a mate.

Butterflies use their colors as *camouflage* to hide from their enemies. The underside of this Small Tortoiseshell is dark. This helps it blend into the background.

Most butterflies feed on nectar. Nectar is a sweet liquid found in flowers. It has sugar in it and gives butterflies the energy they need to fly. Butterflies find the flowers by sight and smell. Like this Brimstone, they suck the nectar through their proboscis.

Some butterflies feed on things other than nectar. This Comma butterfly enjoys the juices from ripe fruit. Other butterflies have stranger tastes. They will suck liquids from rotting animal flesh. Others will draw needed salts from damp soil — or from the sweat on your arm!

↑

These Peacock butterflies are feeding on a buddleia plant. This plant is such a favorite with butterflies that it is also known as a butterfly bush.

While feeding on flowers, butterflies accidentally pick up pollen on their heads. The butterflies then carry the pollen with them from flower to flower. This is very important to gardeners, because it ensures that the plants will become *pollinated*. Pollination is the way flowers produce fruit and seeds to make more flowers.

Courtship and Egg-laying

There are four stages in the life of a butterfly:
1) the egg; 2) the *larva*, or caterpillar, which has
no wings; 3) the *chrysalis*, or *pupa*; and 4) the
adult butterfly.

Courtship and mating lead to egg-laying, the first
stage. A male butterfly finds and chases the
female. The female is attracted to the male by a
special smell. Like these Common Blues,
butterflies mate with the tips of their abdomens
joined. ⬇

After mating, the female looks for a place to lay her eggs. This Cabbage White female is laying her eggs on a plant leaf. The eggs are glued firmly to the plant, and they are laid in a group. The eggs hatch at about the same time. The new baby caterpillars often eat the eggshell for their first meal!

Butterfly eggs are often patterned or have ridges. They are not smooth like birds' eggs.

The Caterpillar

Caterpillars begin to eat as soon as they break out of their shells. Their bodies are divided into three parts, like the butterfly's: head, thorax, and abdomen.

Caterpillars have three pairs of legs on the thorax and usually four pairs on the abdomen and a pair of claspers on the back end. Some, like this Comma, are covered with spines. They help protect the caterpillar from *predators*.

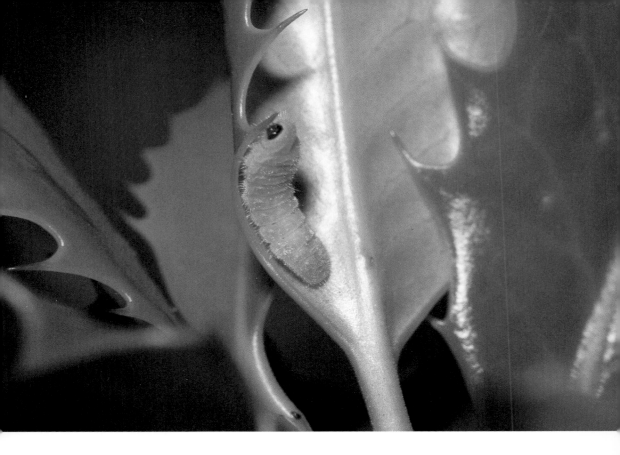

Like this Blue butterfly caterpillar, some caterpillars look like slugs.

Caterpillars spend most of their time eating. Using their strong jaws, they chew and chew until only the ribs of the leaves are left. Some caterpillars are *cannibals*. Others are predators and feed on other insects.

As caterpillars grow, their skin becomes tight and they shed it to grow bigger. This is called *molting*. Caterpillars molt several times.

Chrysalis to Butterfly

Before its final molt, the caterpillar hangs upside down from a plant.

After the skin has split, not a caterpillar, but a smooth, legless chrysalis appears.

Inside the chrysalis, the caterpillar changes into a butterfly. This change is called *metamorphosis*.

The chrysalis has split, and a wonderful thing has happened! The butterfly is now fully formed, and it is coming out.

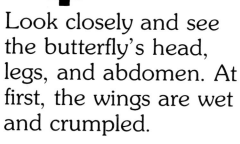

Look closely and *see* the butterfly's head, legs, and abdomen. At first, the wings are wet and crumpled.

The butterfly hangs upside down as the sun dries its wings. Blood pumping in the veins also helps straighten out the wings.

Some butterflies take over a year to grow from egg to adult. Others take only a few months in warmer weather. Like this new Comma, adults do not grow any more once they are out of the chrysalis. All the butterfly's growing takes place at the caterpillar stage.

Migration

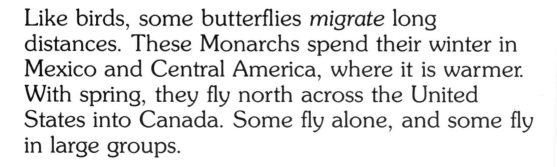

Like birds, some butterflies *migrate* long distances. These Monarchs spend their winter in Mexico and Central America, where it is warmer. With spring, they fly north across the United States into Canada. Some fly alone, and some fly in large groups.

In autumn, Monarchs fly back to the southwest U.S. and Mexico. When birds migrate, the same birds return south in autumn, with their young. With butterflies, usually only the next generation flies south.

Some European butterflies migrate, too.
Butterflies like the Painted Lady (below) spend
winters in North Africa and the south of France.
In the spring, they migrate to northern Europe.

Sometimes migrating butterflies stop, mate, and
lay eggs. The butterflies that emerge will then
finish the trip north. Some butterflies in the main
group finish the trip all the way north, however.

Look closely at this Painted Lady. The hind wings
are damaged a little bit. Perhaps it has just
finished a long flight.

Enemies

The butterfly has to watch out for enemies. Plants and flowers attract many kinds of insects, including butterflies. And these insects attract many animals that eat insects. Frogs, toads, lizards, and small mammals like this mouse eat butterflies when they can catch them. These animals usually cannot catch butterflies in flight. But they can catch butterflies when they are at rest.

Caterpillars are also in danger in the garden. They are food for ants, birds, lizards, and other animals. *Parasitic* wasps may lay their eggs inside the caterpillar. The wasp larvae then eat the caterpillar. These wasp grubs are emerging from inside a caterpillar.

Adult wasps can attack butterflies in flight, and spiders catch them in their webs. This Yellow Crab spider has caught a butterfly which landed to feed on a flower.

Luckily, butterflies lay many eggs. Many butterflies die before becoming adults, but some are always left to start the next generation.

How Butterflies Protect Themselves

Bees can use their sting to protect themselves. Butterflies are not like bees, however. Butterflies can *do* nothing to defend themselves. But they have many less active ways of protecting themselves. Most butterflies use camouflage to hide from their enemies. This Brimstone (above) looks like a pale green leaf. Its wings are even shaped like leaves. The Peacock butterfly's wings (below right) are dark and dull underneath. They help it blend in with the bark on this tree trunk.

The first protection of butterflies is their good eyesight, however. Once they see danger, they can use their wings to fly away. Butterflies can fly zig-zag. This makes it hard for animals to catch them.

Camouflage may not always keep enemies away. The Peacock that blends in so nicely with the tree (below) has another trick it can use. It can quickly open its wings to show four large markings. These markings look like the *eyes* of a bigger animal. They often scare away the butterfly's enemies.

Bright red and yellow on the wings sometimes means that a butterfly is poisonous or tastes bad. Some butterflies do not really taste bad, but they *look* like poisonous butterflies. These butterflies use *mimicry* to fool their enemies.

How the Early Stages
Protect Themselves

Caterpillars also have many ways of protecting themselves. Just like butterflies, brightly colored caterpillars, like this Monarch, taste bad. Predators quickly learn that they are not good to eat.

Caterpillars eating leaves do not have to move very far for food. Birds look for movement in the grass, and they might not notice the slow-moving caterpillar.

This Swallowtail caterpillar can push out two threads from behind its head. These smell bad to attackers. Other caterpillars have hairs or spines which make them hard to eat. Others are camouflaged to blend with their surroundings. Some feed only at night. In the daytime, they hide near the ground.

The chrysalis stage cannot move to escape danger. Like this chrysalis of the Orange tip butterfly, it must use camouflage to protect itself.

Butterflies and Humans

People have always been interested in butterflies. We enjoy their bright colors and patterns, and we have often wondered about their life history. Even today, butterfly patterns decorate our books, walls, and clothing.

It is sad that most of the harm done to butterflies is caused by humans. When we clear land for crops or houses, we also destroy the wild habitats of butterflies and other animals.

People use *pesticides* to kill insect pests. Useful insects are also killed, however, including the bees and butterflies which pollinate flowers. Weedkiller and fertilizer can also hurt butterflies. Both weedkiller and fertilizer help certain plants grow. But they do this by cutting down on many of the other plants butterflies use for food.

We can help butterflies survive by planning gardens with lots of flowers, a few wild spots, and very few chemicals. Butterflies are the insects we notice most in an area. If we make a garden safe for butterflies, we are also making it safe for bees, ladybugs, and other useful insects.

Friends and Neighbors

Many animals share gardens with the butterfly. Many other insects, such as bees and these hoverflies, feed on nectar. Wasps and other insects share rotting fruit with butterflies.

Birds come into the garden at all times of the year. In the spring, birds can find grubs, worms, and caterpillars in the ground. And in the summer, they can catch full-grown insects in flight.

Squirrels compete with birds at bird feeders, and mice, voles, and foxes come out to search for food, mainly at night.

↑

The larvae of many insects, like these sawfly larvae, share the stems and leaves with caterpillars.

Slugs are found in many gardens. They feed on plants at night.

↓

Food Chain

As you can see (below), garden animals need each other for survival. Caterpillars and butterflies eat plants. These insects then become food for other insects and small animals. And these small animals are eaten by larger animals, which return energy to the soil by passing waste or dying.

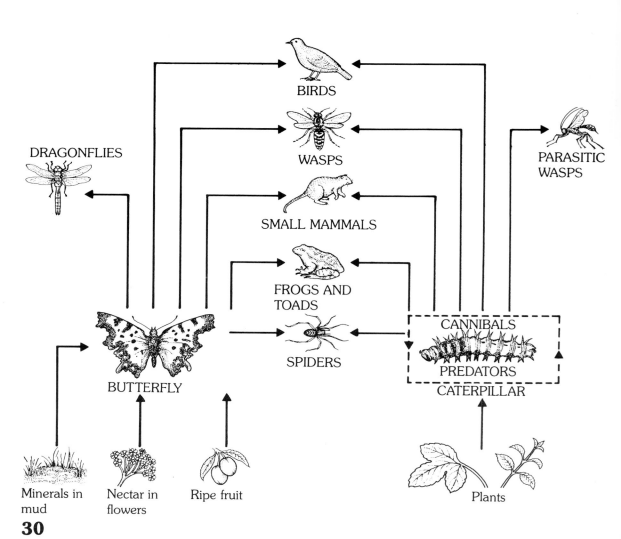

BIRDS

DRAGONFLIES

WASPS

PARASITIC WASPS

SMALL MAMMALS

FROGS AND TOADS

CANNIBALS

SPIDERS

PREDATORS

BUTTERFLY

CATERPILLAR

Minerals in mud

Nectar in flowers

Ripe fruit

Plants

Life in the Garden

The use of land for farming and building has changed many of the natural habitats of butterflies. We can help butterflies survive by saving our natural areas. Even in our parks, yards, and gardens, we can help by leaving patches of wildflowers.

Butterflies flying in a garden or yard tell us that this is a good place for wildlife.

Index and New Words About Butterflies

These new words about butterflies appear in the text on the pages shown after each definition. Each new word first appears in the text in *italics*, just as it appears here.

For a free color catalog describing Gareth Stevens' list of high-quality children's books, call 1-800-341-3569 (USA) or 1-800-461-9120 (Canada).

Reading level analysis: SPACHE 2.2, FRY 3, FLESCH 82 (easy), RAYGOR 3, FOG 6, SMOG 3

Library of Congress Cataloging-in-Publication Data

Saintsing, David.
    The world of butterflies.

    (Where animals live)
    Summary: Simple text and photographs depict butterflies feeding, breeding, and defending themselves in their natural habitats.
    1. Butterflies—Juvenile literature. [1. Butterflies] I. Oxford Scientific Films. II. Title. III. Series.
QL544.2.S24 1986   595.78'9   86-5706
ISBN 1-55532-097-X
ISBN 1-55532-072-4 (lib. bdg.)
North American edition first published in 1987 by
Gareth Stevens Children's Books, 1555 North RiverCenter Drive, Suite 201, Milwaukee, Wisconsin 53212, USA
U.S. edition, this format, copyright © 1987 by Belitha Press Ltd. Text copyright © 1987 by Gareth Stevens, Inc. All rights reserved. No part of this book may be reproduced in any form or by any means without permission in writing from Gareth Stevens, Inc. First conceived, designed, and produced by Belitha Press Ltd., London
The Butterfly in the Garden, with an original text copyright by Oxford Scientific Films. Format copyright by Belitha Press Ltd.

Printed in the United States of America. Series Editor: Mark J. Sachner. Art Director: Treld Bicknell. Line Drawings: Loma Turpin. Design: Naomi Games. Cover Design: Gary Moseley. Scientific Consultants: Gwynne Vevers and David Saintsing.

The publishers wish to thank the following for permission to reproduce copyright material: **Oxford Scientific Films Ltd.** for pp. 3 *above*, 6 *above*, 7, 8 *below*, 9 *below* 10, 11 *above*, 12, 13 *below*, 14 *both*, 16 *all*, 17 *both above*, 20, 22, 23 *both*, 28, 29 *below*, and *back cover* (photographer G. I. Bernard); p. 26 (photographer David Wright); p. 17 *below* and *title page* (photographer Gordon MacLean); p. 2 (photographer Ian Moar); pp. 3 *below*, 4, 6 *below*, 13 *above*, 21 *below*, 24, and 29 *above* (photographer J. A. L. Cooke); pp. 5, 9 *above*, and 25 *below* (photographers J. S. and E. J. Woolmer); pp. 11 *below* and 18 (photographer M. P. L. Fogden); p. 15 (photographer A. C. Allnut); p. 19 (photographer Peter Parks); p. 21 (photographer Derek Bromhall); p. 25 *above* (photographer D. M. Shale); p. 27 (photographer Raymond Blythe); p. 31 (photographer Paul Whalley); **NHPA,** p. 8 *above* (photographer Stephen Dalton); **Animals Animals,** *front cover* (photographer Patti Murray).